Walks on
Islay

Clan Walk Guides

Walks
on the
Isle of Islay

Mary Welsh

First published Westmorland Gazette, 1996
Revised Edition Published by Clan Books, 1999

ISBN 1 873597 13 4

Clan Book Sales Ltd
Clandon House
The Cross, Doune
Perthshire
FK16 6BE

Printed by
Cordfall Ltd, Glasgow

Foreword

I welcome this opportunity to write, at her invitation, the introduction to Mrs Welsh's descriptive book of Islay walks. She kindly discussed the routes with many of the island's owners and those who occupy the land, thus providing interesting and environmentally friendly trails.

I believe that we all have the same aims, namely to enjoy our beautiful island and its uniquely varied scenery while encouraging the traditional industries, wildlife and country sports that it still supports in an ever-changing world. Walking is by far the best way to see and appreciate the countryside and all it represents.

I wish Mrs Welsh and her Islay book the same success as the others in her series.

James Morrison
Director,
Islay Estates Company

Acknowledgments

Islay enchants all its visitors, including me. My grateful thanks go to the many people who helped in producing this book: my friend Maureen Fleming, who walked, researched and checked in her efficient way; Christine Isherwood, who produced the delightful illustrations and maps; Stephen Kennedy, the factor of Dunlossit Estate, who gave me invaluable help and guidance; James Morrison of Islay Estates, who kindly wrote the Foreword; Geoffrey Fitzjohn, also of Islay Estates, who made many useful suggestions; and Thomas Wilks, who made me welcome. The following kindly farmers helped me with routes and gave me useful advice: Hamish McTaggart (Kintra), Hengist Montgomery (Ghiol), Robert Ebbs (Ardnave), Mary MacAllaister, Ian Henderson, and Mary Merrill (all of Portnahaven), Sally Underwood (Carraig Fhada), Gilbert McCormick (Gearach), James Brown (Octomore, Port Charlotte). Thanks also to James Roy (Port Charlotte) and C & E Roy (Bowmore); to Caledonian MacBrayne ferry company for their good advice; and finally to my husband Tom for his continued support.

Author's Note

Please remember on all these walks:

Wear suitable clothes and take adequate waterproofs.

Walk in strong footwear; walking boots are advisable.

Carry the relevant map and know how to use it.

Take extra food and drink as emergency rations.

Carry a whistle; remember six long blasts repeated at one minute intervals is the distress signal.

Do not walk alone, and tell someone where you are going.

If mist descends, return.

Close all gates. Respect walls and fences.

Keep all dogs under strict control. Observe all 'No Dogs' notices - they are there for very good reasons.

Readers are advised that while the author has taken every effort to ensure the accuracy of this guidebook, changes can occur after publication. You should check locally on transport, accommodation, etc. The publisher would welcome notes of any changes. Neither the publisher nor the author can accept responsibility for errors, omissions or any loss or injury.

Location Map

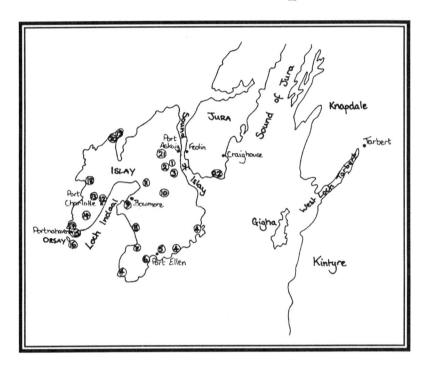

Contents

1. A Linear Walk from Ballygrant to Port Askaig

Information

Distance:	3 ½ miles one way
Time:	A half-day excursion
Map:	Pathfinder 411 Ballygrant and Port Askaig, Landranger 60 Islay, reference 399658 (parking)
Terrain:	Easy walking all the way.

During November, December and January on Mondays to Saturdays, the road into Dunlossit Estate may be signed as temporarily closed owing to shooting and forestry activities. Please adhere to such notices.

Start this delightful walk from the small linear village of Ballygrant. At the southern end stands a row of houses built for workers who mined for lead around the village.

Take the turn, signposted Mulindry, opposite the village shop and park in a lay-by, on the left just beyond the first left turn. Walk back to take this turn, now on your right, and continue to the second entrance, on the left, into the deciduous woodland of Dunlossit Estate.

Stride the firm track to come beside Loch Ballygrant, with its *crannog* (man-made island). A pair of mute

Mute Swans

8

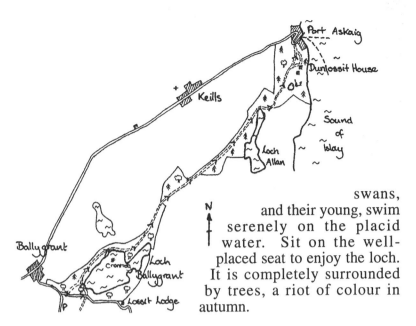

swans, and their young, swim serenely on the placid water. Sit on the well-placed seat to enjoy the loch. It is completely surrounded by trees, a riot of colour in autumn.

Stroll on the pleasing way, from where you can see the village of Keills, away to the left. This small village lies close to its ruined medieval church. It also has the shaft of an ancient cross. In the early 19th century, houses were built for linen weavers from the mainland, to work on flax grown locally.

Continue on the lovely way to pass Lily Loch, its surface almost covered with white water lilies. To the east side, banks of heather pleasingly slope down to the water's edge. Look for a heron hunched on the branch of a low-growing stunted tree, both attractively framed by a row of conifers.

Leave this pleasant scene and climb gently. At the top of the slope a glorious view, across to the Sound of Islay to the Isle of Jura, awaits. Go on to pass through the deer gate. Keep to the main track and stay well to the left of Dunlossit House, which lies to your right.

At the T-junction, do not take any right turns and continue downhill to the cattlegrid at Gate Lodge. Beyond, turn right and descend to the small harbour of Port Askaig. Here you will find a shop and a hotel. From the port, the Jura ferry travels back and forth and the Caledonian MacBrayne car and passenger ferry calls. Here, too, the Islay lifeboat is based.

Jura and the ferry, Port Askaig

You may wish to return by the same route through the magnificent woodland. Or you may prefer to use Islay Coaches, service 451, which returns relatively frequently. For information, telephone 01496 840273.

2. A Woodland Walk to Loch Ballygrant

Information	
Distance:	2 miles
Time:	1 hour
Map:	Pathfinder 411 Ballygrant and Port Askaig, Landranger 60 Islay, reference 396664 (parking)
Terrain:	Easy strolling.

See special note for Walk 1.

Park in Ballygrant. Take the narrow road, signposted Mulindry, opposite the village shop. After half a mile, turn left into the private road of the Dunlossit Estate. Continue past two openings on the left into woodland. Go on to turn left into the wide driveway of The Kennels and walk on in front of the field gate, now the home of the head forester. The house here is built on the site of Islay's oldest distillery.

Loch Ballygrant

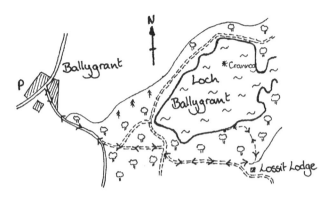

Continue ahead to take a path through the idyllic deciduous woodland. A lively stream dances beside you. The path leads to the side of Loch Ballygrant, and on to end at a boathouse. Pause here to enjoy the lovely loch. Look for dabchicks, mute swans, tufted duck and heron. In autumn, large flocks of fieldfare and redwings descend to feast on rowan berries.

Return by the same route.

3. A Linear Walk from Lossit Farm to the Sound of Islay

Information

Distance:	4 miles
Time:	2-3 hours
Map:	Pathfinder 411 Ballygrant and Port Askaig, Landranger 60 Islay, reference 413655 (parking)
Terrain:	Easy walking to the barn. Steepish climb up and down to the broch. Roughish walking to the shore and to the waterfall.

See special note for Walk 1.

This delightful walk takes you over good tracks, for most of the way, from Lossit Farm on the Dunlossit Estate to the shore of the Sound of Islay. There are wonderful views for all the way and especially from Dùn Bhoraraig, Islay's only Iron-Age broch.

Leave Ballygrant by the road signposted Mulindry. Take the first left turn and drive along the Dunlossit private road. Follow the signposts to park just beyond Lossit Farm, on a wide grass verge, well clear of any gate.

Before you set off, read the notice to hill walkers, which reminds you that stalking takes place on the estate from August to February. It asks you to check at the farm that it is safe to walk.

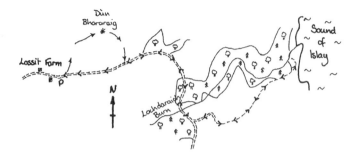

Enjoy the fine view of Loch Lossit, which is surrounded by mixed woodland and set in a quiet hollow in the rolling hills. Pass through the gate and continue to the next one, along a track walled on your right. Beyond, climb left, up the hill, and continue climbing until you reach the cairned summit of Dùn Bhoraraig (619 feet). Here,a large pile of stones is all that remains of the galleried tower, 50 feet in height. It is believed that it was constructed around 100 BC to AD 100. Little remains today, but there are traces of a gallery, entrance and circular outer wall. Enjoy the glorious view of the Paps of Jura and of the whole length of the Sound. To the north, you can see the mountains of Mull. To the south, over Gigha and the Mull of Kintyre, the Arran mountains stretch along the skyline. To the west is the west coast of Islay, clearly visible on good days.

Buzzards circling

Descend the steepish slopes to rejoin the track and stride on. The way is lined with summer flowers and in the pastures on the right large numbers of rooks flock, unworried by a pair of circling buzzards.

Follow the track as it winds downhill, passing through beds of yellow iris. Continue towards a sturdy barn, where rock doves fly off. Go along the reinforced track, keeping the barn to the right. The way soon becomes grassy and then for a short time disappears. Press ahead in the same general direction until a good track appears.

14

As you come close to mixed woodland, follow the way to just beyond the last two birch trees and then leave the track, left. A grassy swathe, through bracken, heads towards the shore. To your left, you can hear only the Lochdaraich burn as it descends noisily over its bed. It is hidden from sight by

The Paps of Jura from Dun Bhoraraig

dense vegetation. Near the shore, in high summer, the rough path is lost under high bracken, but press on to the pebble beach. Sit here and take in the views and the sights of the seals and of the Jura ferry crossing the Sound. If you wish to view the waterfall, stroll up through the glade, beside the burn. You will have to go in Spring, before the bracken takes over and it becomes too difficult.

Return the same way. Remember, it is all uphill.

4. Three Short Walks

Information

Distance:	Kildalton Cross and Church 1 mile
	Dunyveg Castle ½ mile
	American Monument 1 mile
Map:	Landranger 60 Islay, reference 454508
	(Kildalton); 407457 (Dunyveg); 282423
	(Monument).

Do not attempt the walk to the American Monument in the mist. If mist descends, return immediately.

Visiting Kildalton Cross and church, Dunyveg Castle and the American Monument involves short distances that provide an exciting glimpse of Islay's past.

Kildalton Cross

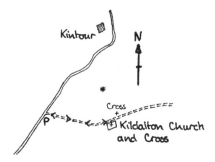

To reach the oldest of the three sites, the famous ninth-century High Cross of Kildalton, drive on the A846 through Port Ellen and continue for seven-and-a-half miles. The historic site is signposted and there is a small car park, set in glorious deciduous woodland, nearby. Walk the narrow road as directed. In pasture on either side, dragonflies loiter in the sun over bog myrtle, scabious and clumps of heather. As you approach the church, look for a sparrowhawk as it flies low, threading its way among the trees.

The cross stands in the graveyard of the ruined Kildalton Church. The weathered cross is carved, probably by a sculptor from Iona, from one piece of local grey-green epidiorite. It is a ringed cross with its arms intact. Look for the sacrificial scenes, and the Virgin and Child with attendant angels, carved into the east face.

Dragonfly (Golden ringed) on Devil's bit scabious

Kildalton Cross

Go inside the 12th- or 13th-century church, the walls and gable ends of which are still standing. Look for the fine grave-slab with an effigy of a knight in armour. Outside in the graveyard look for more slabs. Enjoy this glorious corner, where sycamores shade the walled cemetery. Cross the narrow road to see a smaller late medieval cross, standing in a railed enclosure. Nearby you might see red deer and several rather dark fallow deer. There is a small car park by the church. Return along the road to rejoin your car.

Dunyveg Castle

Drive back along the main road for four-and-a-quarter miles. Just before the first house on the left, at Lagavulin, take an unsignposted left turn that leads towards a short grassy track to Dunyveg Castle. This crumbling, unstable, romantic ruin, with not much more than a corner of its keep still standing, dates from the 17th century, with traces of an earlier castle still visible. It provided a safe, well-hidden anchorage for the ships of the Lords of the Isles.

Across the charming bay stands the Lagavulin Distillery, one of three to be found in this part of Islay. It produces a single malt whisky. Look for its two pagoda roofs, which ventilate the malt kilns.

American Monument

To visit the American Monument, return through Port Ellen and take the left turn to the left of its distillery, signposted Mull of Oa (pronounced O). Follow more signposts for five miles, up a narrow road with passing places, to park in a small car park at the gate to the access track to Upper Killeyan Farm. Here you are invited to pass through the gate and to follow the markers. You are reminded that all dogs must be on a lead.

The pleasing one-mile walk is well waymarked. Stiles take you through fences, and duckboards carry you over wet areas as you near the top of the high cliffs. The massive monument draws you on. Its sad legend seems even more poignant set on this austere, lonely outpost of Islay.

The monument commemorates 650 American sailors and soldiers, who died in two naval disasters in the closing months of the First World War. Many of their bodies were washed up at the foot of the cliffs.

From this high point, on a clear day, you can see the coast of Ireland. Enjoy the magnificent view south-east along the fine coastline but take extreme care on the sheer unfenced cliffs. Not only dogs, but children should be under close control.

Before you leave, look north along another glorious part of Islay's coastline; across Loch Indaal to see the lighthouse off the Rhinns and the villages of Port Charlotte and Bruichladdich. Return over the moorland by your outward route.

5. A Circular Walk from Port Ellen

Information

Distance:	3½ miles
Time:	1½-2 hours
Map:	Pathfinder 439 Port Ellen, Landranger 60 Islay, reference 367453 (parking)
Terrain:	Easy walking.

The houses of Port Ellen curve around its shapely bay, sheltered under The Oa. It is Islay's biggest village, has its own distillery, and is also the main ferry terminal for the island. Walter Frederick Campbell, the laird, started to build the village in the 1820s and named it after his first wife Eleanor.

Wander along the attractive seafront and then set off on this pleasant walk along mainly narrow roads, just north-east of Port Ellen.

Hare

Walk with care for nearly a mile along the road to Ardbeg. Notice the fine walls that edge the road, constructed with their stones placed vertically, rather than horizontally, as is more usual.

Just after the mile-stone, turn left before a large white house, to

20

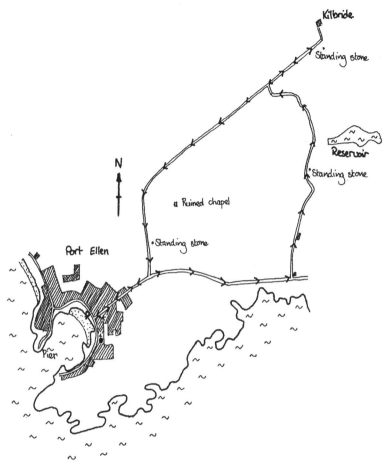

walk a narrow ascending rough road. After half a mile, look for a standing stone on your right. Beyond, lies the blue water of a reservoir where tufted duck and wigeon idle in the sun. Go on along the lovely lane as it flattens out with moorland pastures on either side. Here, a hare races over the rough grass.

At the T-junction, turn right to walk to the end. Look right to see another sturdy standing stone up on a small hill. Return to the T-junction and continue ahead along the virtually traffic-free road. Just beyond where it swings left to join the main road, look left to see yet a third standing stone. Ponder

Third standing stone,
near Port Ellen

here on how these might have been used as ancient man's calendar. Enjoy the extensive views of the Mull of Kintyre, with the mountains of Arran beyond.

At the lane end, turn right to return to Port Ellen.

6. A Linear Walk to Carraig Fhada Lighthouse and Singing Sands

Information

Distance:	2 ½ miles
Time:	1-2 hours
Map:	Pathfinder 439 Port Ellen, Landranger 60 Islay, reference 345456 (parking)
Terrain:	Easy walking.

This short walk is full of interest and provides enjoyment for all the family. On the way you visit a moving memorial by one of the island's lairds to his wife.

Leave Port Ellen by the road that runs left of the distillery, signposted Mull of Oa, and follow it for a mile. Ignore the right turn to Kintra, and less than a quarter of a mile further turn left to park on the sandy turf, just beyond a fine deciduous woodland.

Walk down towards Kilnaughton Beach, a beautiful stretch of yellow sand. At the shore, walk left to view a fine, but now roofless, bathing hut where once John Ramsey's family walked

Corn marigold and meadow sweet

23

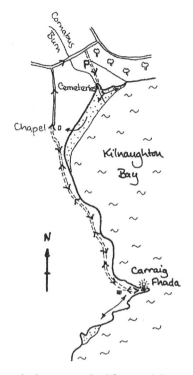

from their house, Cairnmore, through woodland to bathe. It is set into the cliff, with heather-covered crags on either side and woodland above.

Return along the sands and cross Cornabus Barn at an easy place. Look here for mute swans, ringed plovers, curlews and gulls - their footprints covering the shore. As you near the graveyard, walk right to join a good track leading to the ruins of the 13th-century chapel. Look inside for a carving of a knight.

Continue along the good track, which runs in the direction of an unusual lighthouse. The track is lined with summer flowers. Here you might see thrift, golden rod, corn marigolds, yarrow, tormentil, heather, meadow sweet, silver weed and wood rush. From here too can be seen the Mull of Kintyre and the Arran tops.

Follow the track round to pass in front of Carraig Fhada Farm, where there is a craft shop. Take the concrete and bridged causeway to the fascinating solar-powered lighthouse, Carraig Fhada. It was erected in memory of Lady Eleanor Campbell, who died in 1832, by the laird, her husband, Walter Frederick Campbell.The view here of Port Ellen, named after Lady Eleanor, is delightful.

Go on along the signposted way for the Singing Sands, taking note of the signs about dogs and about closing gates. Walk the lovely stretch of white sand, along which are scattered strangely tortured, heavily eroded outcrops. The sands are given this name because of the sound the wind

Carraig Fhada

makes blowing over the grains. This is the place to idle.

Return by the same route. At the graveyard, continue along the road, inland, where on the left you might see a fine herd of Highland cattle. Turn right at the Oa road to rejoin your car.

7. A Circular Walk from Kintra

Information

Distance: 4½ -5 miles
Time: 3 hours
Map: Pathfinder 439 Port Ellen, Landranger 60 Islay, reference 321483 (parking)
Terrain: Easy walking to Tockmal. Could be wet until you reach the cliffs. The return walk could also be wet and challenging. Walking boots essential. Carry waterproofs.

This grand walk has all the best that Islay has to offer: a standing stone, three deserted townships, an ancient chapel, cup-marked rocks, a magnificent stack, a natural arch,a deep spectacular chasm, two waterfalls, otters,seals, eagles, choughs, wild goats, natural woodland and sandy bays.

To reach the start of the walk at Kintra Farm, turn left at Port Ellen distillery onto Oa Road, following the Kintra road sign for two-and-a-half miles. Park through the gate to the left of the path from the Old Granary Restaurant at the farm. With your back to the restaurant, follow the track to the left that winds above the shore. Look right to see the glorious seven-mile strand edging Laggan Bay. Ahead, across the mouth of Loch Indaal, you can see the lighthouse on Orsay, off Portnahaven.

Pass through the gate, on which a notice says, 'No dogs beyond this point'. Follow the good track, a former drove

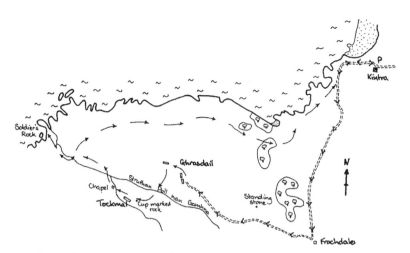

road, as it moves steadily out into moorland, where bog myrtle, rush, heather, bog asphodel, grass of Parnassus, marsh St John's wort, yellow mountain saxifrage and scabious grow. As you climb steadily, birch and willow thrive in the native woodland to your right and, away to the left, the hill slopes are planted with young conifers.

Then the birch, willow and huge banks of heather crowd the right side of the track. Look for boletus toadstools, brown and white and brown and yellow ochre, below the birch. The track leads you towards the ruined crofthouse of Frachdale, high on the moorland. It has grand views but is in a very exposed position.

Just before the ruin, follow the track right and climb steadily. As you approach the gate in the fence, look right to see a tall standing stone. Pass through the gate and keep to the sometimes indistinct green track as it moves ahead through heather moorland. Aim for the ruined township of Ghrasdail. Look for the kiln, set into the slope on your right, before you reach the roofless dwellings. Here, a pair of buzzards and their young lazily take flight, causing a commotion among the hooded crows.

Descend steadily left, passing remnants of old walls, to cross the narrow stream, Sruthan Poll nan Gamhna, flowing

27

through the glen. On its shallow banks grow irises, water mint and rushes. Just before Tockmal, another ruined township of several crofthouses, look for a boulder with several small depressions. Such boulders are known as cup-marked rocks. Continue to a narrow tributary of the main stream, on your left. Step across at a suitable place, to look for traces of the sanctuary chapel and graveyard, in summer almost completely hidden by bracken; Tobar an t-sagaert (Priest's Well) marked on the OS map is now not traceable.

Go on towards the shore, crossing the main stream to avoid some very wet walking. Just before it enters a deepening gully, cross back again. From here great care should be taken, especially if children are walking. The stream tumbles in small falls and then, as the gully becomes immensely deep, it drops elegantly over stepped rocks to plummet far below.

Proceed along the gully edge to cross above a natural arch. From here there is a spectacular view of Soldier's Rock, a fine stack with glistening veins of quartz. Below, where the cliffs drop sheer to the water, is a deep pool, Slochd Maol Doiridh. Sit on the cliff-top turf and enjoy the view of the wild coastline. Watch for choughs, glossy black birds, cousins to a raven but smaller. They

Soldiers Rock

glide gracefully just below you, their beaks brilliant red in the sunshine. Then up they fly, uttering their distinctive call 'kee-ow'.

Below, too, sit a row of shags, drying their outstretched

wings. A pair of lesser black-backed gulls sunbathe on a nearby stack. Watch the eider duck families braving the waves as they learn to swim.

Leave this idyllic corner by the way you approached and then head on, east, along the coast, keeping high up above the

Choughs

shore, but still with pleasing views. Follow helpful sheep trods over the high, pathless moorland. Continue for a little more than a mile, before you begin to descend. To do this you must find a way that suits you and which you find easiest. There is no set path.

Just before you reach the quartzite cliffs at Port Alsaig, you will need to find a way through the natural birch woodland; again, go the way the sheep go. Continue around two sandy bays, edged with conical shaped grassy peaks to reach a good farm track. Soon after joining it, head left to the cliff edge again and walk on to see a pretty waterfall on the Abhainn Ghlas.

Rejoin the track and cross the burn on convenient stones or a footbridge upstream. Join your outward track and turn left to rejoin your car.

8. A Circular Walk around the Airport

Information

Distance: 4 miles
Time: 2 hours
Map: Pathfinder 424 Portnahaven and Port Charlotte,
            Landranger 60 Islay, reference 332515 (parking)
Terrain: Very easy. Tricky part, crossing the ford.

This walk has been described as a fun walk, with something for all the family. It takes you close to Islay's tiny airfield, along a glorious stretch of Laggan Bay —— 4¾ miles of golden sand, over flat, easy-to-walk tracks, and through a ford.

Park opposite the terminal building, where there is a wide expanse of open ground. Cross the road and walk south for 100 yards in the direction of Port Ellen. Take a grassy track leading off right and follow it as it heads towards the shore. The path comes to the side of the Machrie River, where you might be able to cross on convenient stones, or you might have to wade.

Beyond, follow a track to a gate ahead (ignoring the airport gate, which

Great northern divers

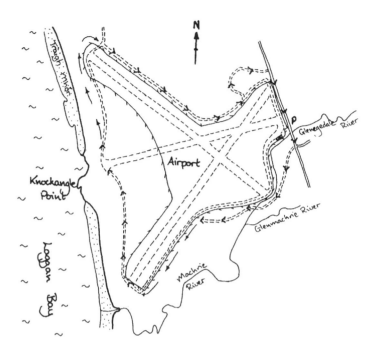

carries a notice stating that there is no entry). Stroll on where the track bears left and then follow it as it heads right along an old runway, above sand dunes, with the blue waters of Laggan Bay stretching away into the distance. Half-way along this section of the walk is Knockangle Point, the supposed site of the first inn on Islay.

Continue on along the asphalted surface. Towards the end of this section, you can gain easy access to the lovely stretch

Laggan Bay

of golden sand without walking through the dunes. Look here for eiders, common gulls, redshank, curlew, great northern divers and black-throated divers. Once past gate five, bear right and follow another wide track, another old runway, and on to the road. Here you might see a small private plane take off, one of many that use the airport. Or you might see a Shorts 360, operated by Loganair under franchise from British Airways, providing the scheduled service between Islay and the Mainland and other islands.

Turn right, walk to the terminal building and cross the road to rejoin your car.

9. A Circular Walk from Bowmore

Information	
Distance:	8 miles
Time:	4 hours
Map:	Pathfinder 424 Portnahaven and Port Charlotte, Landranger 60 Islay, reference 312597 (parking)
Terrain:	Generally easy walking, but walking boots advisable.

Bowmore is Islay's attractive capital. It has spacious wide streets and a pleasant square with several bench seats. Stand at the bottom of the main street (by the square) and look up to the splendid round Kilarrow parish church with its octagonal tower and stone cupola, built by Daniel Campbell in 1767. Go inside and enjoy its peace. Look for the pulpit fall and the wonderful old photograph.

Golden plovers

Park in the free car park or at the side of the street leading up to the church. After visiting the church, turn left as you leave and follow the road for Port Ellen. At the end of the bonded warehouse, an extension of the MB Distillery, turn right. At the T-junction, bear left to walk a quiet hedged lane, where on a still day you can see pleasing reflections of Bruichladdich and Port Charlotte.

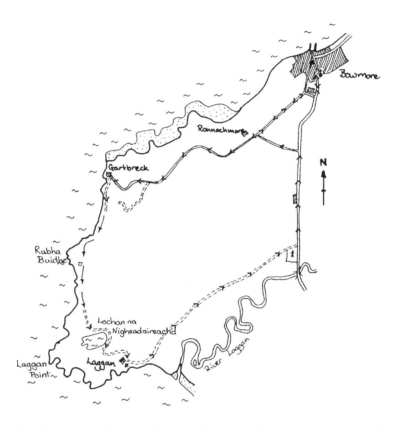

Continue past Ronnachmore Farm and on along the track, which in autumn is lined with heather, golden rod, scabious and bramble. Pass Gartbreck landfill site, which is well-screened from view. Keep to the path, now no longer metalled. At a junction of tracks, take the right branch to walk towards the ruined Gartbreck Farm and follow the track as it swings left along the shoreside of a fence. Look for oyster-catchers, wigeon, bar-tailed godwits, golden plover, lapwings, redshanks and curlews probing the sands. Then watch for a peregrine flying low over the shore and putting up all the birds in a most spectacular way.

Pass through a gate close to the shore. Huge mounds of seaweed cover the rocks. Stride the glorious turf, where harebells and mushrooms grow. Overhead, a pair of choughs fly uttering their strange cry.

Head towards a ruined building to pick up a good track with grand views over the tortured Torridonian rocks lining small bays. Out to sea you can glimpse the hills of Ireland.

Follow the track as it swings left towards Lochan na Nigheadaireachd and continue left around the shallow, partly reed-covered sheet of water. Stroll the track towards Laggan, passing the house and farm on your right.

Walk on beside Port Ghillebride and pass through the once-gated wall. Ignore the track to your right and continue on the partly - reinforced way, where heather moorland stretches away to the left and the River Laggan hurries through its tree-lined banks to the right. After a mile, as you near the road, the way becomes pleasingly hedged and then wooded.

Bowmore Church

Turn left and walk with care the road to Bowmore. After three-quarters of a mile, you might wish to leave the road and turn left along a grassy, hedged track towards Ronnachmore. On joining your outward narrow road, turn right and retrace your earlier route from Bowmore.

Before you leave, walk down to the jetty.|Offshore in the spring and winter months, look for common scoter, Slavonian grebes, eiders, mergansers, scaup, whooper swans and red-throated divers.

10. A Linear Walk to Dùn Nosebridge

Information	
Distance:	1½ miles
Time:	1 hour
Map:	Pathfinder 411 Ballygrant and Port Askaig, Pathfinder 425 Bowmore, Landranger 60 Islay, reference 364598 (parking)
Terrain:	Easy walking but strong shoes required.

The quaint name of this dùn encourages you to seek it out. The name is believed to be a corruption of a Norse word that means a fort on a crag - an apt description. The walk to the dùn is a delight.

From Bridgend, take the narrow road signposted Mulindry and drive for two miles. Pass Neriby House and then a cottage. Drop down a slope and park in a lay-by on the left, before the narrow Mulindry Bridge. The gate to the track to the dùn also lies on the left, immediately before the bridge.

Walk the track, which is shadowed by hazels, with a tiny tributary of the Laggan Burn to your right. At the division of the track, take the left branch and continue into oak and birch woodland, the haunt of chaffinches, siskins, coal, blue and long-tailed tits. As you emerge from the

Siskins

37

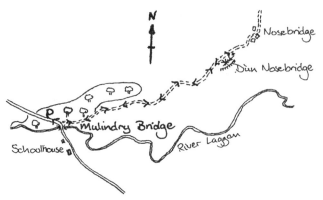

trees into an open area, look left to see more oak woodland stretching up the slope.

Ahead, on a long raised crag, stands the dùn. Keep to the higher of the two tracks and continue past the fort. Turn right, and an easy way to ascend the ramparts and ditches is seen. Take care on the south-eastern side, where a steep cliff falls sheer to the flat land below.

What a view from the top over the flat rolling moorland and pastures! What a defensive position! Beyond, hills lie to the west and higher hills to the east. Over a hump to the south you can see the sea. Overhead a pair of buzzards circle, filling the air with their calls.

On your return to Bridgend, park in the lay-by in front of the church on the right, just before the village. Cross the road and pass through the gate to visit the John Francis Campbell monument on the hill. He was the son of Walter Frederick Campbell and was a scholar, linguist, scientist and traveller. Stand at the foot of the obelisk for an extensive view of Loch Indaal and of the countryside around.

Dùn Nosebridge

11. A Circular Walk from Bridgend

Information

Distance:	5½ miles
Time:	2-3 hours
Map:	Pathfinder 410 Bruichladdich and Bridgend, Landranger 60 Islay, reference 336625 (parking)
Terrain:	Pleasing easy walking.

This walk starts at Bridgend, a village that lies near the head of Loch Indaal. It has several shops, petrol pumps, toilets and a pleasant hotel. On the outskirts of the village, deep in trees, stands Islay House, until recently part of the Islay Estate. This was built by an 18th-century Campbell laird. He objected to having his view obscured by the village of Kilarrow and moved those villagers who did not work on the estate to Bowmore, pulling down their houses.

This walk takes you through the delightful deciduous woodland of the estate, close to the River Sorn, returning by a narrow road above Loch Skerrols.

Park outside the village shops and cross the road. Walk left and continue in the direction of Port Askaig, following the tree-lined road with care as it bears right. Look for yellow balsam flowering in a ditch, together with

Dipper

39

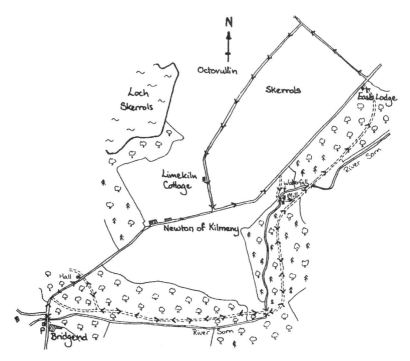

spearwort. Notice the variety of ferns thriving in the roadside walls. Opposite a rather shabby building on your left marked 'Hall' on the map, take the small white gate beside a large locked one. This leads into pleasing woodland.

Pass below limes and sycamores. When you reach a T-junction of tracks, bear left and saunter on for nearly a mile along the lovely way. Here you might see bullfinches, siskins, tree creepers, goldcrests and coal tits.

When the track divides, take the left fork and continue to a large stile to a track, which you cross. Stride on over the bridge above the River Sorn and walk on to East Lodge.

Beyond the lodge gate, turn right, cross the road and take a hedged track leading off left. Climb gently to a T-junction, where you turn left to walk the vehicle-free narrow public road. This high-level way takes you through pastures, where sheep and cattle graze, and gives you a grand view of Loch Skerrols, almost surrounded by woodland.

Pass Limekiln Cottage on your right and then look left to see a tall-fronted limekiln. At the road to Ballygrant, turn left and walk for a quarter of a mile. Turn right at the sign for the woollen mill. Descend to the bridge and look left to see the Sorn's turbulent waterfall, the haunt of dipper, heron and grey wagtail. You might also be lucky to see an otter or a kingfisher.

The Woollen Mill and River Sorn

To the right, beyond the bridge, stands the old waulkmill, a building where the women sat round a large table pounding the linen, woven from flax grown close by. On the left is the mill, where you can see weaving in progress. The mill was built in the late 19th century and there is some machinery of a similar date. You might also find time to visit the well-stocked shop.

Go on up the hill to a large wooden stile, on your right, taken earlier. Climb this and retrace your outward route, remembering to turn right twice to rejoin the road, opposite the old hall. Turn left to walk back down the road to Bridgend.

12. A Circular Walk from Port Charlotte

Information

Distance:	4 miles
Time:	2 hours walking time
Map:	Pathfinder 424 Portnahaven and Port Charlotte, Landranger 60 Islay, reference 254586 (parking)
Terrain:	Strong shoes or boots for the walk over Octomore Hill.

Port Charlotte, a pretty white-washed village, has a tiny harbour and an extensive view across Loch Indaal to Bowmore and down to the Oa peninsula. The village began to be built in 1828 and was named after Walter Frederick Campbell's mother.

Combine a visit to the village with a walk over the pastures above, where another magnificent view awaits. Park in the car park on the left as you enter the village from Bridgend. Cross the road to visit the excellent Museum of Islay Life, housed in a converted church. Opposite is the Port Charlotte Creamery, where Islay cheese is made, using milk produced by the island's cows.

Return to the road and walk on into the village, to visit the delightful Islay Field Centre situated in Port Charlotte's former distillery warehouse. Beyond the centre, turn left and walk towards the shore. Bear left along the sands and over rocky outcrops, continuing, over two stiles, to the wall of the lighthouse. The lighthouse stands on a dolerite dyke. Look for

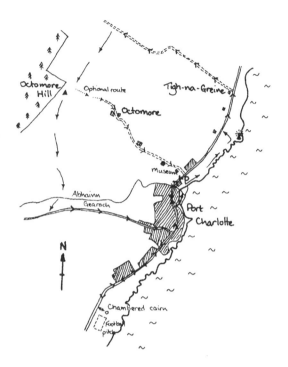

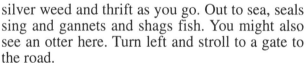

silver weed and thrift as you go. Out to sea, seals sing and gannets and shags fish. You might also see an otter here. Turn left and stroll to a gate to the road.

Turn right and walk along the road, with glorious views across to the sea loch. Once past a house named Tigh-na-Greine, turn left to walk a good cart-track, which is lined with blackberries in autumn and where wild mint, pink convolvulus, meadow sweet, wild iris and purple loosestrife thrive.

Where the track divides, take the left branch to pass through a gate and go on along the way. Overhead a pair of buzzards circle. Beyond the next gate, walk on until you can just glimpse the

Purple loosestrife

tops of the sitka spruce in the plantation ahead.

Look left to see the gate at the junction of a wall and a fence and choose the driest way, through bog asphodel, over the pasture. Beyond the gate and stile, climb steadily to Octomore Hill, from where you can often see Ireland. Here you have a choice. You may decide to descend a clear track to pass to the left of Octomore Farm. As you go, look for the nest hole for choughs built into the chimney of a holiday cottage on your left. Follow the track downhill to rejoin your car.

Alternatively, continue the walk from Octomore Hill, striding on over rough ground, keeping to the left of a large grassy mound.At the junction of a fence and a wall, pass through a stile over the fence on your left. Descend steadily to the boundary fence, where you bear left to pass through a gate. Head downhill towards a telegraph pole and then on down again and then on down again to cross the Abhainn Gearach. Climb diagonally right to a gate to the road.

Turn left and saunter along the narrow road towards Port Charlotte. Turn right at the main road and continue past the last house. Go through the gate on the left to walk across the end of the football pitch. Here stands a chambered cairn, a Neolithic burial site, divided into two chambers.

Return towards Port Charlotte and turn right to walk along the edge of the bay to see the small pier. Go on through the village to rejoin your car.

Port Charlotte

13. A Circular Walk from Gearach, West of Port Charlotte

Information	
Distance:	3 ½ miles
Time:	2 hours
Map:	Pathfinder 424 Portnahaven and Port Charlotte, Pathfinder 410 Bruichladdich and Bridgend, Landranger 60 Islay, reference 223594 (parking)
Terrain:	Hard walking on parts of this walk. Could be very wet. Walking boots essential.
No dogs allowed.	

This tough three-and-a-half mile trek is a delightful challenge. After passing a 20th-century dam, which holds the water of Loch Gearach, the walk takes you back in time to various periods of the island's history. You visit a 19th-century ruined village, then a Bronze-Age standing stone, before finally travelling forward in time again to climb a 3rd-or 4th-century dùn.

Leave Port Charlotte by the narrow road signposted Kilchiaran. Continue for two miles to park on a grassy verge, on the right, just beyond the access track to Gearach Farm. Walk back along the road to take a track on your left, leading towards Loch Gearach. Follow the track as it swings right and cross the Abhainn Gearach on boulders.

Climb ahead steadily to pass through a gate. At a junction of narrow paths, take the branch leading off right. Continue along this as it climbs a small hill and then descends to cross a wet area - a little bog-hopping is required here. Go on along the clear path and follow it as it continues north, with Loch Gearach below to the left.

The path leads deep into the quiet, lonely heather moorland. Look for honeysuckle clambering over willow. Here, bracken and heather compete, together with crowberry. Keep to the right of a stone enclosure and press on. The path is now indistinct. Aim for the first of the ruined houses of the deserted village of Grimsay. Wander around the old buildings, taking care as you cross the rough tussocky pasture. From here, you can glimpse the Atlantic.

Pause to watch for a pair of eagles circling slowly overhead, steadily and effortlessly rising higher until they are lost from sight. From the village, look left (west) to see a standing stone. Then make your way towards it, choosing the easiest way and stepping across a narrow feeder stream of the reservoir.

Stand by the ten-foot high lichen-clad stone to obtain a good view of Grimsay. Then look south (the direction of the loch) to see a small conical hill, Dùn Glas an Loin Ghuirm. Walk on to visit it. While standing on the

Golden eagles circling

excellent vantage point, where sea pinks, tormentil and scabious flower, look right (west), to see the corner of fencing edging a plantation of spruce. This is the way to continue.

Walk towards the corner, choosing the driest way and negotiating a small stream. Go left (west) to another fence and follow it right, staying with it as it turns left and steadily descends to a good track. Turn right and follow the way to the road, where you have parked.

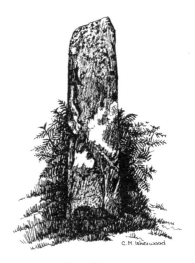

Standing stone

14. A Linear Walk over the Rhinns of Islay

Information

Distance:	4½ miles
Time:	2 hours
Map:	Pathfinder 424 Portnahaven and Port Charlotte, Landranger 60 Islay, reference 188556 (parking)
Terrain:	Easy walking all the way.

Beyond Port Charlotte lie the Rhinns, a high flattish moorland where peat is cut. Much of the land has been planted with sitka spruce. From the Atlantic comes a sharp tangy breeze. Gaelic is spoken in Port Charlotte and on the promontory. The area is now managed by the farmers and landowners in conjunction with Scottish Natural Heritage.

This quiet, easy linear walk from the west coast of the promontory to the east starts on the west coast road, south of Lossit Farm. Park just along the track, making sure not to obstruct the way, which is used by the post van and forestry workers.

No directions are needed. As you go, enjoy the ever-changing views of the island and of Kintyre, Arran and Ireland. The track is edged by a ditch colourful with wild flowers. Fortunately the conifers have been

Hen harrier

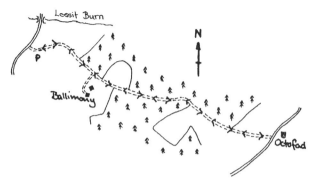

planted well back from the track and a wide swathe of heather thrives on either side.

Listen for robins and wrens among the trees. Watch for a hen harrier flying low and direct after a flock of twittering meadow pipits. Notice the peat moor where the fuel has been cut by hand and by machine.

The walk ends at the A847 by Octofad Farm. On your return, enjoy all those views you missed on the outward route. As you return to Port Charlotte, park in the large lay-by at Kilchiaran. Here, visit the signposted, partially restored medieval church, possibly of 14th-century origin. It is dedicated to Ciaran, one of the monks who accompanied St Columba. Go inside to see the font, and several grave

Kilchiaran Church -
Font and grave slabs

50

slabs that have been brought in from the graveyard. Drive on for a short distance to pause by the next farm building. Look for a semi-circular winnowing barn where power was once provided by a huge wheel turned by the flow of the burn.

15. A Walk round Port Wemyss and Portnahaven

Information

Distance:	1½ miles
Time:	1 hour
Map:	Pathfinder 424 Portnahaven and Port Charlotte, Landranger 60 Islay, reference 167519 (parking)
Terrain:	Easy walking all the way.

At the end of the Rhinns peninsula stand twin villages, Portnahaven and Port Wemyss, divided by Rainich Burn. To reach the snout of this windswept promontory of rough ground and mixed farming, drive along the A847 until you reach Portnahaven's primary school, on your left. Turn left here and continue to the sea, where you turn right. A hundred yards along , after crossing the burn, park on the left in a large lay-by, beyond the track to the pier.

Walk back the way you came. Ignore the left turn and walk ahead in front of the delightful cottages, several with

Portnahaven

52

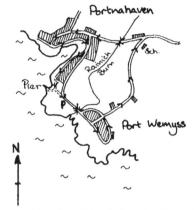

well-cared-for gardens on the shore side. Across a narrow channel is the island of Orsay, with its towering white lighthouse.

At the corner of the narrow road, there is a magnificent view across Loch Indaal to The Oa. The laird, Walter Frederick Campbell, began building Port Wemyss in 1833. He named it after his father-in-law, the 8th Earl of Wemyss.

Follow the road round to join the road to the primary school, where you turn left. This leads you over the dividing burn and into Portnahaven, built in 1788 by Walter Campbell, grandfather of Walter Frederick Campbell.

Descend to the shore, from where you have a pleasing view of the picturesque houses lining the narrow creek. They stand on rock that in several places falls sheer to the water and they face each other across the bay. Common seals haul out on rocks and a large grey seal swims close by. Shags sit on other rocks and sandpipers call from the shore.

Seals basking at Portnahaven

53

Walk round the creek, passing in front of the cottages. No two are alike. Continue beyond the last house at the western point and go on to pass the small pier. Stride on the track to the road to rejoin your car.

16. A Walk on the Island of Orsay

Information

Distance:	1 mile
Time:	1½ hours
Map:	Pathfinder 424 Portnahaven and Port Charlotte, Landranger 60 Islay, reference 167519 (parking)
Terrain:	Generally easy, but off the paths it is hard walking on the tussocky grass. Walking boots advisable.

The lighthouse on the island was built in 1824. Ask Alistair MacArthur of Portnahaven, a local boatman, to take you across the channel (10 minutes), weather permitting. Walk the carefully tended paths and wander the grassy pastures. Visit the medieval chapel of St Columba; one gable end and four

Gannets fishing

sturdy walls still stand.
Stroll with care around the
island; some gullies drop
unexpectedly to a great
depth. Notice the fog horn,
neatly painted but now no
longer in use.

The lighthouse is in
pristine condition, the
brickwork white and the
woodwork a soft ochre
yellow. Inside all is well
tended. The brasses gleam.
The view over the Rhinns, from the top, is
extensive.

Talk to the keepers about the birds seen.
In times gone by the lighthouse keepers
recorded sweeping up barrow-loads of
birds that had been lured to their deaths by
the light. Today, with a
different beam, there
are far fewer fatalities.

On the island, shags
and most of the gulls

Orsay Lighthouse and end of St Columba's chapel

breed. Look out to sea to see gannets hurrying by and cormorants flying up the channel. Here, too, in this narrow stretch of water you should see common and grey seals.

Make sure you are waiting on the jetty for your pre-arranged departure time.

17. A Circular Walk from Portnahaven

Information	
Distance:	3½ miles or 4½ miles
Time:	2 hours or 3 hours
Map:	Pathfinder 424 Portnahaven and Port Charlotte, Landranger 60 Islay, reference 165522 (parking)
Terrain:	Generally easy.

This is a delightful walk along the north-west shore from Portnahaven, which gives you the opportunity to visit a glorious sandy bay and view the experimental wavepower station.

Beach with wave machine

Park tidily near the north-west corner of the bay. Walk north, in front of a row of attractive cottages, with the shore to your left. Just before the last house, heed the notice and turn left to the shore. Turn right, and follow a narrow path to a fence where a notice says 'No dogs'. The way takes you along the pleasing short-cropped turf, between outcrops of gneiss.

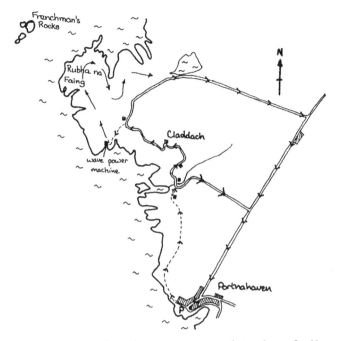

Here grow many lovely waxcap toadstools, of all colours from bleached and creamy through to deep red. Look along the shoreline for a cave. Across the narrow channel lies Mackenzie Island, a neighbour to Orsay and its lighthouse.

Press on over a huge bay of large, wave-rounded boulders, picking the easiest way. Aim for a small gate in the fence, put there to aid walkers. Pass in front of the crofthouse and go on to the edge of a small inlet where turnstones feed. Follow this round right to join a narrow road.

Stroll left, to cross a small bridge. Climb the winding road to pass Claddach and walk along the high-level way to a small green gate just before the next house. Pass through and drop down the slope to a delightful sandy bay. Look for large clumps of sea holly. This increasingly rare plant has prickly leaves and pale blue flowers, tightly packed, rather like a thistle head. The leaves have a waxy blue coating that protects them from the effects of sea spray.

Follow the narrow path round the bay and then towards the large concrete housing of the wave power machine. After reading the explanatory notice, do not be tempted to go out onto the ramp - it is extremely slippery and the water is deep and choppy.

Cross the small footbridge behind the machine and note the comments about access. No dogs are allowed. Continue on the short turf above the riven shore, where sheep graze. Look across to Frenchman's Rocks, lying offshore. This area is much favoured by bird watchers. Here you might see hundreds of guillemots flying south in small groups and storm petrels flying low over the waves and quite close into the shore.

Sea holly

Press ahead , taking great care as you go around the sheer-sided and steep gullies. Climb the stile over the fence by the second gully and head inland to join the narrow road by a small loch, where you might see red-throated divers and whooper swans.

You might prefer at this point to take the shorter route back by turning right and retracing much of your outer route, turning right at the T-junction to return to Portnahaven. If you wish to make it a longer walk, turn left and stride the long straight virtually traffic-free lane to the T-junction. Turn right and stride another long straight road to return to the village.

After rejoining your car, you may like to drive the road just walked. It continues through a pleasant part of the island, with grand views over the rocky coastline and out to sea. Here on nearby cliffs you might see choughs. You might also see a stag grazing close to the road.

18. Machir Bay and Kilchoman

Information

Distance: 2½ miles

Time: As much time as you have

Map: Pathfinder 410 Bruichladdich and Bridgend, Landranger 60 Islay, reference 209636 (parking) 218634 (Kilchoman Church)

Terrain: Easy walking over the sands.

Machir Bay is not a safe swimming beach because of the currents.

To reach the lovely strand of yellow sand, drive the narrow road overlooking Loch Gorm, Islay's largest freshwater loch where, in fields in the autumn, barnacle and Greenland white front geese feed. The moor about the delightful sheet of water stretches away like a patchwork quilt made of soft golds, greens and browns. To this loch vast numbers of white-fronted, grey lag and barnacle geese return each autumn.

Where the road turns sharp left towards Kilchoman, continue ahead down a pebbly track and on towards the sands, to park on a grass verge.

Barnacle geese

From here, walk the mile-long strand, which is

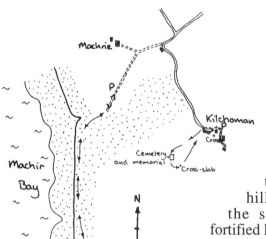

overshadowed on the landward side by sand dunes. Look for the green path leading onwards, beyond the point where jagged outcrops of slate and grit jut seawards. Go on towards the nearest hillock on the right, the site of a dùn or fortified hill.

Return from here along the sands. As you drive from Machir Bay, turn right to continue uphill to Kilchoman. Park near the dilapidated, structurally unsafe, but still striking church. Near here the Lords of the Isles had their summer residence.

Kilchoman Cross

Walk into the churchyard to see the 14th-century cross, erected by John, the first Lord of the Isles. Look for the carvings of Christ, with Mary on his right, surrounded by saints and angels. The reverse side has intricate carving. The pedestal has four hollows, in one of which is an oval stone. Turning the latter was thought to help a woman give birth to a son. The churchyard, too, has some fine medieval grave-slabs.

Leave the churchyard and walk back along the

road to a stile beyond the second cottage. Take note of the sign if the bull is there. A path leads over the pasture to a walled cemetery. Here, rows of identical gravestones commemorate those members of the crew of *HMS Otranto* washed up on the shore. The ship was lost off Islay on 6th October 1918 - a month before the Armistice was signed. Standing tall, above this moving sight, is a stone monument supporting a sword.

As you return to the stile, walk right to a small mound of stones to see an upright stone slab engraved with a cross, perhaps marking the site of a chapel.

Before you leave this glorious corner, look up on the cliffs, where choughs are known to breed.

19. A Circular Walk around Ardnave Point

Information

Distance:	4 miles
Time:	2-3 hours
Map:	Pathfinder 397 Ardnave Point, Landranger 60 Islay, reference 286728 (parking)
Terrain:	Easy walking. Odd patches of damp ground.

Ardnave Point lies at the tip of a large low-lying sandy promontory, which juts out into the Atlantic. On it grow some marram and much grassland, which provides grazing for a large number of sheep and cattle. It is partly sheltered by Nave Island and several smaller islands against which break gigantic rollers. To its east is the wide entrance to Loch Gruinart, where the tide races in. On the ebb, its extensive expanse of sand is revealed. Once the loch stretched further inland but the land has steadily built up at its head.

Take the narrow road, well-signposted, in the direction of the RSPB reserve at Aoradh Farm. In 1984 the society

Nave Island

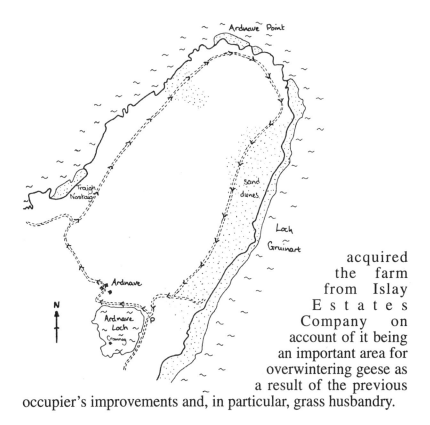

acquired
the farm
from Islay
E s t a t e s
Company on
account of it being
an important area for
overwintering geese as
a result of the previous
occupier's improvements and, in particular, grass husbandry.

Here, turn right for Ardnave, which lies three miles along
the narrow road. Park just beyond the cattle grid beside
Ardnave Loch. Look for the crannog towards the far side of
the loch, where a pair of herons stand, vigilantly watching for
prey. Here, too, a mute swan preens, and wigeon, mallard,
teal, tufted duck and dabchicks idle. On a very small island, a
flock of peewit rise, calling their name. In autumn many geese
feed around its shores and sometimes an otter is seen.

Follow the track around the loch in the direction of Ardnave
Farm, a listed building with a crenellated barn beyond. Pass
between the two buildings and bear left to go through a gate
to stride left, where the track moves out over rolling
grassland. Ahead lies the Atlantic.

The track swings right and then takes you above the dunes. Cross a wet gulley, where grass of Parnassus grows with scabious, wild mint and ragged robin. Look for red admiral butterflies flitting about the harebells. Pass through a gateless gap in the fence and head towards the shoreline for a good view of Nave Island, with its ruined chapel. Close to it is a chimney that was built when fish were cured here. Beyond the island you can see Colonsay, eight miles away. Listen here for the haunting 'singing' of seals hauled out on the island.

Walk with care over the layers of grits and slates tilting towards the sea. Stroll on around the coast, where lady's bedstraw, scabious and small-flowered crane's bill prettily colour the turf. On the shore ringed plovers

Otters - adult and cub

and oyster-catchers seek for food. Look for otter tracks across the sand. Continue round the headland to look across the bay towards the hills of northern Islay.

Watch for shags, cormorants, terns, eiders and innumerable gulls as you go. Pass through the gap at the end of a boundary fence, close to the shore. Then begin to move inland, keeping above the enormous dune system along this eastern side of the promontory. Join a track heavily marked with tractor wheels and follow it through a gate. Look left to see the Paps of Jura, peeping over the northern hills.

Just before the track swings right, you can see the roof of a building on the shore. This was once a herring curing station. Continue on the way to return to Ardnave Loch and your car.

20. A Linear Walk from Ardnave Loch

Information

Distance: 6 miles (to the boundary and back)
Time: As much as you have
Map: Pathfinder 397 Ardnave Point, Landranger 60 Islay, reference 286728 (parking) 283716 (Kilnave Chapel)
Terrain: This is a more challenging walk than the previous one, once you have passed the stone circle. It can be wet in parts.

Park as for Walk 20. Stride the track through Ardnave Farm and walk on until it swings right, near to the Atlantic shore. Here, turn left, and stroll the short-cropped turf. Continue across the bay, or walk inland round the bay, depending on the tide. Go on over a stretch of pebble beach and then for a short distance (100 yards) over rough pasture, which could be wet. Look under the low crags, on your left, for a stone circle. Here, several squat stones stand proud and others lie flat. There is some doubt that this is an ancient circle.

Press on along the grass and heather tops of the slates and grits, which jut fearsomely out to sea. Look for dykes that cut across the beach and into the waves. Keep well inland away from the narrow deep ravines that slash the shallow cliffs.

Merlin

67

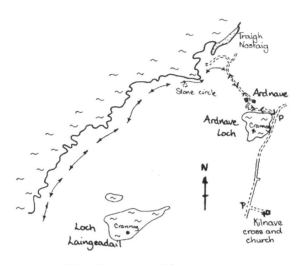

Enjoy this wild riven coastline, a great contrast to that around Ardnave Point, seen on the previous walk. Walk for as far as you wish, which could be to the boundary fence. Return by the same route

For the second part of this walk, drive a mile from Ardnave Loch, along the road used to approach it, and park in a lay-by on the right. Opposite, take the gate to a track that leads to the ruin of the 12th-century Kilnave Chapel. A visit to this medieval gem is a must for all visitors to Islay.

Look for the 8th-century standing cross, still magnificent though parts of its arms are missing and much of its intricate carving is badly weathered. Go through the low entrance, which is arched with thin slabs of stone, and savour the peace within. Then wander round the older part of the graveyard to look at the simple 18th- and 19th-century stone slabs embedded into the turf.

Kilnave Cross

Pause in this lovely corner of Islay. Listen for the mournful calls of the seals and the more buoyant piping of the waders from the sandy flats of Gruinart Bay. In winter, geese graze the surrounding pastures.

As you enjoy this delightful corner of the island, it is difficult to believe that in this chapel 30 men from Mull, followers of MacLean of Duart, were burnt to death. The followers of Islay's Sir James MacDonald believed that MacLean's army had murdered their chief, and exacted this terrible revenge.

21. A Linear Walk to Finlaggan

Information

Distance: 3 miles
Time: 2 hours
Map: Pathfinder 411 Ballygrant and Port Askaig,
Landranger 60 Islay, reference 403677 (parking)
Terrain: Easy walking.

The MacDonald Lords of the Isles ruled much of the west coast of Scotland and the islands. They administered their vast kingdom from Finlaggan, which was the home of the chiefs from the 12th to the 16th century. Here they met, as equals, the kings of England and Scotland.

If driving from Port Askaig, turn right at the sign for Finlaggan and park tidily at the side of a remnant of the old road on your right. Walk the narrow road, towards Mulreesh. It is lined with alder, rowan, willow and ash. Continue on as the way swings right to pass through moorland. In September, the verges support large numbers of the delicate grass of Parnassus against a colourful background of hardheads, field scabious, ragged robin, yellow vetch and corn marigold.

Grass of Parnassus and knapweed

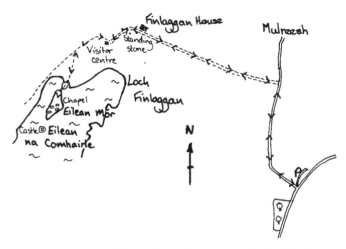

Where you turn left at the signed track for Finlaggan, the narrow road goes on to Mulreesh, an area where lead and some silver were mined.

Stride the track towards the historic site, watching for Loch Finlaggan to come into view. It lies in a quiet hollow among hills, where sheep graze. To the west of the loch, some of the heather moorland has been planted with conifers. On a dull day, when a slight mist fills the air, this site has a magical, mysterious aura.

Go past Finlaggan House and look for the broad, squat standing stone opposite. Turn left to walk to the well-organised and interesting interpretative centre, housed in a restored cottage. It was opened in 1989.

Pass through the small gate on the right and walk right to join a reinforced path, which leads to duckboarding and a small boat, provided by the Finlaggan Trust for access (a few yards) to Eilean Mór (the big island). Here stand the gable ends of a hall and a chapel, the latter believed to have been founded by St Findlugan, a companion of St Columba. Look for the beautifully carved gravestones, one of a knight in armour and a ship. The Trust hopes to construct a shelter within the chapel for these glorious relics, once the chapel has been consolidated. It is believed that wives and children were

71

interred here, but the chieftains were buried on Iona.

From the west end of the island, remnants of a more modern causeway lead to Eilean na Comhairle, where the Lords are believed to have held their council, within a sturdy castle. This island and one further south, are crannogs. The southern one is believed to have been used as a prison.

Finlaggan

To obtain details of opening times of the interpretative centre, telephone 01496 850273.

Return by the same route.

22. A Walk through Jura House Garden and to the Misty Pool

Information

Distance:	4 miles
Time:	2 hours
Map:	Pathfinder 411 Ballygrant and Port Askaig, Landranger 60 Islay, reference 488638 (parking)
Terrain:	Generally easy, but walking boots advisable for the walk along the cliffs and shore.

Guide books can be obtained at the noticeboard, where the reasonable entry fee is paid. The garden is open all year round. For information telephone Jura 315.

On many walks on Islay, Jura's presence is felt. The Paps, Jura's conical-shaped mountains, draw the clouds, leaving Islay free to enjoy fine weather. So the author includes this

Islay from Jura - Tràigh Bàn

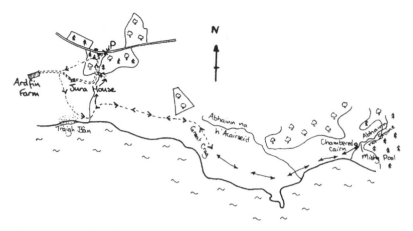

fine excursion in the hope that walkers visiting Islay will enjoy a day over the Sound.

Take the vehicle and passenger ferry, Western Ferries (Argyll) Ltd, from Port Askaig on Islay to Feolin on Jura. Turn right and drive the main road for five miles to Ardfin and the car park for Jura House. The Campbells controlled the island in the 18th century and they built the house. Today it is owned by the Riley-Smith family.

From the car park, cross the road and pass through the gate. Walk the good path through rhododendrons and deciduous trees. Continue to the noticeboard and follow the signs for 'Garden Only'.

A gate in the 12-foot high enclosing wall admits you to this quiet, secluded oasis on Jura's south shore. The garden was laid out a hundred years ago and during the last twenty years the head gardener, Peter Cool, and his small team, have developed and cosseted it.

Wander at will to see the wide variety of plants that flourish here. The garden has an extensive range of Australian and New Zealand plants, all of which thrive in the mild and frost-free climate.

Outside the wall, on the shore side, is a wild flower garden beside a pond. In a greenhouse and shade tunnel, plants are produced for sale. During the summer months you can obtain refreshments, and there is a toilet.

Take the shady path just before the shade tunnel and descend the good stepped way beside a narrow ravine. Near the end of the path, look for sheets of liverworts covering the wall of rock to your left. These are growing on Jura's narrow band of slate, which was once mined at Tarbert and Inverlussa, though it was never commercially viable.

Cross a little bridge and continue on towards the lovely sandy shore of Tràigh Bàn - the sands are 'singing sands' when scuffed with your shoes, like those found on Colonsay and Eigg. Enjoy the magnificent view across the Sound to Islay, where you have a good view of MacArthurs Head lighthouse.

Go on left through a dry-stone wall. It stops, on the seaward end, in a natural black dyke, formed of epidiorite (the same rock as that from which the Kildalton Cross was carved). This dyke is named Crab's Rock. Cross two footbridges where wild fuchsias grow against the wall of a tall cliff. Walk along the pebbly beach, which is composed of fine-grained hard quartzite.

Then follow the long flight of steps up the cliff, with a huge rock-face of quartzite to your right. The track winds right at the top, where you continue ahead for a viewpoint and perhaps to make use of the picnic table. Look right, up the Sound, to see Heather Island,with its ruined Claig Castle, now just a stump on a crag. The island has the sea on three sides and a deep channel between it and Jura, making it an impregnable site for the fortress of the Lords of the Isles, who demanded tribute from all those who passed through the Sound. The castle also helped to protect the chief's fleet in Lagavulin Bay.

Pass through the gate behind the viewpoint. Turn right and walk along beside the fence. Go on through the next gate - which has a splendid old catch. Follow the high wire fence as it climbs up onto The Great Crag. From here you would once have seen Brosdale, a crofting township that was demolished in the middle-19th century. It spoiled the view from Jura House and the Laird's wife had the community moved to a new village above the main road.

From here, look for the old path winding up from the shore. Crofters carried seaweed up this path to fertilise their land. Look also to see if you can see Colonsay or Ireland. As you walk along the top of the cliff, you step across lazy-beds.

Drop down the slope, with a good view of Brosdale Island. Look for seals here. Over the fence, far down on the shore, you might also glimpse a herd of white goats.

Go on around the bay, keeping above the jagged shoreline, but heading down towards it to cross the mouth of Abhainn na h-Acairseid. Here salt was brought ashore and stored.

Proceed around the bay, following the good sheep-trods, to the far side, where the Abhainn na Sroine flows through a lush ravine to reach the sea. Look up on a flattish area, for two upright stones. This is Jura's treasure, the remnants of a Neolithic chambered cairn, dating from about 2000 BC, where bones were buried after a cremation. Further upstream is another gem, a delightful waterfall that tumbles under rowan, birch and alder into a deep pool, known as the Misty Pool. After rain it lives up to its name.

Return by the same route to the gate by the viewpoint at the top of the long flight of steps up the cliff. Do not pass through the gate, but turn right and walk up the side of the fence. Look left to see Jura House, a grey sturdy house. Pass through the gate into woodland and walk right.

At a T-junction of tracks, turn left and then take the second right to return to the noticeboard. Pass through the lodge gate and turn right to return to the car park. While on the return ferry look right for the Bunnahabhainn distillery tucked into the foot of the hills, set on the shore, north of Port Askaig.

left to see Jura House, a grey sturdy house. Pass through the gate into woodland and walk right.

At a T-junction of tracks, turn left and then take the second right to return to the noticeboard. Pass through the lodge gate and turn right to return to the car park. While on the return ferry look right for the Bunnahabhainn distillery tucked into the foot of the hills, set on the shore, north of Port Askaig.

Clan Walks

A series of walks described by Mary Welsh, covering some of the most popular holiday areas in the Scottish Highlands and Islands.

Titles published so far include:

1. 44 WALKS ON THE ISLE OF ARRAN
2. WALKS ON THE ISLE OF SKYE
3. WALKS IN WESTER ROSS
4. WALKS IN PERTHSHIRE
5. WALKS IN THE WESTERN ISLES
6. WALKS IN ORKNEY
7. WALKS ON SHETLAND
8. WALKS ON ISLAY
9. WALKS ON CANNA, RUM, EIGG & MULL
10. WALKS ON TIREE, COLL, COLONSAY AND A TASTE OF MULL

OTHER TITLES IN PREPARATION

Books in this series can be ordered through Booksellers anywhere. In the event of difficulty write to Clan Books, The Cross, DOUNE, FK16 6BE, Scotland.